1659

811
LEW   Lewis, Claudia
           Louise

           Up in the moun-
           tains

DUE DATE   **BRODART   08/92   13.89**

Up in the Mountains

and Other Poems of Long Ago

Up in the Mountains

and Other Poems of Long Ago

by Claudia Lewis
pictures by Joel Fontaine

A Charlotte Zolotow Book
An Imprint of HarperCollins*Publishers*

UP IN THE MOUNTAINS:
AND OTHER POEMS OF LONG AGO

HarperCollins Children's Books,
a division of HarperCollins Publishers,
10 East 53rd Street, New York, NY 10022.
Typography by Elynn Cohen
1   2   3   4   5   6   7   8   9   10
First Edition

Library of Congress Cataloging-in-Publication Data
Lewis, Claudia Louise, date
   Up in the mountains : and other poems of long ago / by Claudia
Lewis ; pictures by Joel Fontaine.
       p.   cm.
   "A Charlotte Zolotow book."
   Summary: A collection of poems depicting the life of a young girl
in turn-of-the-century America.
   ISBN 0-06-023810-0. — ISBN 0-06-023812-7 (lib. bdg.)
   1. Children's poetry, American. [1. Family life—Poetry.
2. American poetry.] I. Fontaine, Joel, ill. II. Title.
PS3562.E939U64   1991   90-4439
811'.54—dc20   CIP
                                                                AC

To my brothers and sister
And to the memory of
Our brother Bunny
(Ronello B. Lewis)

Contents

To Introduce Our Town

The streets—

There's a trick
about their names—
If you know the streets
that run from the river
up to College Hill,
then you know
the presidents
of our country
in their right order—

Yes, first, Washington, of course,
      then Adams
               Jefferson
               Madison
               Monroe
But
No Adams for the sixth.
What small town could have
two streets named Adams?
So we skip to Jackson
and Van Buren,
way over at the edge of town,
where I seldom need to go.

And now the mountains
over toward the west—

Of course we all know Mary's Peak,
our beauty, our elephant (in shape)
and the highest.

But the one that I like best
is a little hill
I can see above the trees
from our front bedroom window.

There's a clearing
on the slope—a green field—
and a spot
that must be a house.

Who lives there?
I like to wonder.
They never know
I'm watching
from the window.

I stare and stare—
What life goes on there?

Turn the pages, now,
for the life that I live here—

On Jefferson,
number 754.
There's a plane tree
in the parking,
and behind the house
a little maple
my oldest brother planted—
It's growing!

3

My Father's Words

"Our only little girl,
and we're pretty proud of her."

My father's words
as we meet his friends
outside the movie—

Proud of me?

I know
my parents love me,
but "proud"
I've never heard—
And he tells his friends
it's so!

The word
leaps into me
and I become
one big exclamation point
shooting up, up!
all the way home.

5

The Best Birthday Present

From Mother

Four long strips of store-bought cheesecloth, soft and fine,
                in pink and blue, purple and green

Just to wrap around me—
                                Egyptian princess!
Or just for dancing—
                                Dryad from a tree,
                                    an ancient pine!

Mother knew
my favorite game
of draping myself
in old towels
or tablecloths,
whatever came
along, to dress up in—

Now Kate and Jill and I
can dash out to the grassy field
where there's room

to dance the wind,
dance flowers
and queens,
even room to dance Persephone
caught by the god
and carried down
to darkness
while the maidens
scream and run,
maidens in their lovely
pink and blue,
purple and green—

All afternoon
we dance our games
and our capes
are velvet
flowing behind us
as we fly about
on silken wings.

At Mrs. Garner's

I almost wished
there'd be another
San Francisco Fair,
and our parents would travel down
again, and leave us
with Mother's old friend
Mrs. Garner.

Those dinner times!
The two big daughters
and the tall son
would be home from work,
and there we all sat
around the table,
the four of us little kids
among the grown-ups,
and no special conversation
for our sakes.
Instead, we heard
all about Helen's beau
and what he said
and did the night before—
"Shall I, shall I
marry him?" she'd wail,
and everyone would talk about
yes and no.

While grown-up Bill
petrified us, telling
how he nearly drowned
in the river—
how he went down once,
twice, three times,
and how his whole life
whirled past him in his thoughts
as he was leaving it forever.

    Then suddenly
    a man dived in
    and pulled him out!

Whoosh!
Up we went,
we four,
shooting
breathless
toward the future,
listening there
years away,
eating
Mrs. Garner's dinner.

SLAP! SLAP!

Our principal, Mr. Jackson,
is a big, fat man
with curly hair
and lots of smiles—
But—
as he walks around the school
he keeps a wooden paddle
up his sleeve,
sometimes letting it
slip down a bit
so everyone can be sure
it is there.

Has he ever used it?
Maybe not, for years and years—

13

But one day
all of us were sitting
at our desks hard at work
when suddenly
outside down the hall
we heard
        SLAP! SLAP! SLAP! SLAP!
        a wooden paddle, beating
        on a boy?

We looked around at one another-
Our teacher at her desk
just sat—
her mind far away—

Who was it? What did he do?
And was he really paddled?
The truth is
        we never knew.

The Woolen Dress

In fifth grade
Jane was in my class
for a while—
How odd she looked
in her heavy long dress
with double sleeves,
all out of date,
an old-fashioned style.

At recess
the girls were sometimes
a little mean to Jane.
They'd gather round
and tease with questions,
or laugh—
Even I, one day,
wanting to belong
to the gang, dared to ask,
in my soft voice,
"What kind of a dress is that?"

Quiet, friendly,
"It's a woolen dress,"
she said.
I turned away,
ashamed.

So—she thought I was asking
something else entirely—
(Did she?)

Then Jane was absent
for a long time.
And finally
one day at home
my father read aloud
from the *Daily News*
that a little girl
named Jane McEwen
had died.

"Did you know her?"
my parents asked,
upset and sad.

"Yes, she was in my grade,
but I didn't know her
very well"—
That's all I said.

But I was haunted
by her words,
"a woolen dress."
Dear God, Dear God, I prayed,
please let it be
that she never guessed
why I asked,
and what a cruel thing
I meant to say.

"a woolen dress"—
I hugged her words
to comfort me.

Stealing Old Easter Candy
My Brother Was Saving in a Little Box

Stale and old—
But look!
Delectable—
    head of a little
        marshmallow lamb,
    bits of chewy chickens,
    eggs!
        speckled
        pink and purple—

Could I?
I mustn't—
But shall I?
No!
Maybe?

Quick!
Grab lamb
Jump
    back of door
Chew
Chew
Gulp down
    guilt
    lamb
    all one—

Not much fun.
More?
No!

A Little Walk

Angry words?
Our mother
and our father?

They had gone
into the kitchen
through the swinging door,
leaving us—
supposedly—
where we could not hear,
at the dinner table,
eating our dessert.

Broken snatches
came to us—
Our gentle mother
tense and fierce—
"I can't...I won't...
I had enough of this
when I was young...."

Slam!
The outside door
banged shut.
Silence, then,
in the kitchen.

Had they gone out?
No, Father soon
came striding through,
not speaking.

And Mother?
Where was she?
Suddenly
through the window
I saw her—
hurrying down the street,
away—

No, no—
I ran and ran,
reached her,
grabbed her hand,
looked up—

"Oh, dearie, I was just
going for a little walk."

So be it,
if this is what
I must believe.

Around the block
we walked—
our everyday block,
past Johnsons' house
and Moores',
past the low pine
where I had played
in the afternoon—

Then home,
the two of us,
holding on.

One Happy Morning

We knew a baby
was coming,
but Mother didn't tell us
when.

Then—
one morning early,
Papa woke us
on the sleeping porch.
"You have a baby sister!"

My three brothers
let out groans
because it was a girl
and not a boy—

But I—
I jumped up on my bed
and bounced and bounced
and shouted out
for joy.
    (A little girl
    she'd soon be,
    with curls
    and a checked
    pink gingham dress—
    a little girl
    for me to love
    and wheel about
    and play with.)

"Look under your pillows,
everybody," Papa said.
There, for each of us,
a little nest of nickels,
pennies, dimes—
"Mother left it for you,
to spend while she is gone."
More joy! But then—

Papa joked: "We'll call her Bedelia!"
No No we screeched.
"Rosamund, please," I begged,
"or Rosemarie or Beatrice!"
"Well, we'll see."
Still screeching
we got dressed—
Downstairs
our neighbor Mrs. Moore
had come
to help with breakfast,
curl my long curls
on her finger,
and pin the ribbon
in my hair.

   (She didn't know
   the right way—
   She hurt me,
   pulling back
   too far.)

But I must
tell the news
quick, quick!

Across the street
I dashed
to my best friends
and stood there by the steps:

"LILLIAN! EVA!" calling loud—

　　(Tight hair pulling,
　　but who cared
　　on this happy morning in September?)

"LILLIAN! EVA!

WE HAVE A BABY!

I HAVE A BABY SISTER!"

Alone at Night

Never before
left alone—
but tonight they had to return
to the creek—
a quick ride
there and back—
to hunt for the baby's silver spoon
lost in the grass.

Alone in the house,
and darkness of night
falling.
Alone
in my bed,
the brothers sleeping
down the long hall.

Safe?
Of course—
But robbers could
climb ladders
and crawl in?

31

(Guardian Angels,
spread your wings
around me!)

What do I hear?
A creak-creak
on the stair?
A burglar's feet
softly padding
up the steps?

(Angel wings,
surround me!
Let no bullets through!)

I must believe
the wings are here—
I know, I know they are—
Whoever comes to kill me
surely cannot reach me—
keep me, keep me, Angels,
safe!

Suddenly
downstairs
beloved sound—
Front door!
Papa's home
and Mamma—
Here!

No burglars now,
no angels,
no wings hovering—
Only soft night air
stirring.
Mamma comes upstairs—
Already I am sleeping.

Love and Housework

Mother talked with me
about it—

"You say you
love me so,
then why
don't you want
to help me?"

"Love
has nothing to do
with housework!" I raged,
and stamped my feet
and made ugly faces.

Those chores—
    dust the stairs
    set the table
    dry the dishes—
I hated hated hated them.

Then came the morning
when Mother tripped
and fell
against the window
in the cellar door,
ripped her right arm
wide open—

We children hovered
in the dining room
while the doctor
and our father
took care of Mother
in the kitchen.

(Was she lying
on the floor?
Was the doctor
stitching up the wound?
Could she bear it?
Would she die?)
It was very quiet in there.

Suddenly I rushed
upstairs,
made all the beds
carefully,
without a wrinkle;
hung up all the clothes;
in Mother's room
laid the silver brush
and mirror
straight.
What else?
What else could I do for Mother?
(Dear God,
don't let her die.)

Back in the dining room
father came to us—
"Mother's all right,
don't worry—
She wants all of you
to run along now
to school"—

We left,
but on the porch
I stopped a moment
to move the wicker chairs
a bit
and pick up
yesterday's
scattered toys—

The Sad Song

"When I was a little boy
I lived by myself,
and all the bread and cheese I had
I put upon a shelf."

When my father sings
his little short song
it has a sadness
about a boy
who lived all alone.

Himself?
No, it's just a nursery rhyme—
I've known this all along—
And yet
when he sings,
doesn't my father
belong in the song?

A little boy alone,
the song says,
a little boy
who lived by himself on bread and cheese
he kept on a shelf—

Where? How?
My father? No, no!
And yet—could it be?
I know his mother did die
when he was only three.

The tune is sad, the words sad,
and there's a mystery about a little boy
alone, age three—

No, no! It's just a rhyme,
not my father, age three.
But who was the boy alone
long ago
and how old was he?

41

Over the Corduroy Road
to Tillamook

Bump—bumpBump—
Driving to Tillamook
over the mountains—

Now we've come
to the corduroy road—
    logs and boards
      laid down to drive on—

Bump! It's fun
and we're sucking on
hard molasses candy!
    Chewy chunks
    glassy brown—
    Mother made it
    in a pie pan—

Bump! to Tillamook
over the mountains,
Bump! to the rolling ocean—
    Our summer fun
    has just begun!

Summer Beach Days

Plump down
each   bare   foot
in   deep   soft
dunes—
    Jump!

Race along wet beach
a mile maybe—
tide's out—
and climb (watch it!)
those jutting rocks
where ocean swirls below—
    (Dangerous!)

Run—and splatter in waves
spilling foam on the shore—
Poke about, dig,
pick up shells, and stones
with a sparkle—
Explore—
till day's end.

Back then
up the dunes
to our beach home—
    (Breathe
    sweet honeysuckle air)

Home
to supper
on thick white plates
and chocolate
     (delicious)
in tin cups.

Home
to summer beds,
sleep and dreaming,
and in the dark, mysterious night
sound of ocean
roaring.

Up in the Mountains

Visiting My Friends

Waking—

Yes, SUN!
I see it shine
on the trunks
of the giant trees
surrounding us.

Great trees,
you tell me
I'm here
in the mountains—

One look through the window
and it's
Joy!
    for another day
    of the rushing river
    and the waterfall
    where the stream runs
    over rocks—
    and for the path
    to explore
    deep in the woods—

(What pioneers
or miners
lived here
long before?)

Joy!
    for a leaping run
    through morning air
    downhill to the road
    with the sack
    for the mail truck—

Then
    breakfast
    on the porch

        (oven toast,
        and on the oatmeal
        brown sugar, cream)

UP!
    you tell me,
    great trees,
    filling me
    with joy—

I'm up
and rushing OUT!

The Comb of Trees

A Secret Sign Along the Way

Riding to Rock Creek
for our picnics
we swing around
a certain curve
and then I see it—

    Standing high
    on a mountain ridge
    a little row
    of firs, with trunks
    tall and bare,
    lined up one by one—
    a comb
    against the sky.

As we draw near
each time
I wonder—

Is it ... ?
Is it ... ?

Then we turn—

Yes! It's there!

No storm
has wrecked my comb,
no lumberjack
has chopped it down—

All's well
still
(a while?)
up there.